# Your First 90 Days in Network Marketing

by

Angel Olvera

First Edition: November 2015
Printed in the United States of America
ISBN-13: 978-0-9969314-1-0
Published by OmediO Corp

I dedicate this book to you,
because you're just like me.

You want to be successful and
found a way to get it done...

And you deserve to have the
right tools to get it done.

If I did it, you can do it.

# ACKNOWLEDGEMENTS

I would like to express my thanks to the people who have supported me and my dreams throughout the years. There were times when things were tough but with my family and friends pushing me to achieve my goals (and to all the people who said NO to me and fueled my fire) I say thank you for what you did for me. Without it, I wouldn't be able to write this book to help others' dreams become a reality.

I thank my team, the Vision Group. Without you guys being coachable to our team's system, I wouldn't be where I am today.

You guys make me look good.

# Table of Contents

# Chapter 1

# INTRODUCTION

This book is a guideline on what your first 90 days in the Network Marketing world should be. If you're reading this book and just started your journey in Network Marketing, welcome! This industry can change lives and position you and your family on the road to true wealth. Your first 90 days in Network Marketing are critical because they establish your mindset and give you the fuel you need to make a roaring fire. This book will help you develop a skill set that you can duplicate out to your organization to build true residual income. Along with this book and the system your upline has developed, you'll be unstoppable.

If you're reading this book and you've already been in the industry, for a month, or even years, whatever - you can start your first 90 days over. I remember when I went to my first company convention about 30 days into starting the business. That convention blew me away. That's when I got fired up! After the convention is when my first 90 days started. We tell people that you aren't in the business until you go to a convention, because at a convention, you really see what you are a part of.

Don't get discouraged because it's been a year and you don't have the results you want. Just start your first 90 days again, but this time, let's do it the right way.

# MY STORY AND EXPERIENCE

My name is Angel Olvera. I grew up in the unforgiving streets of Los Angeles, California. I don't come from money but I've always wanted to live a lifestyle people dreamt about. I didn't graduate from high school, and before I was even an adult, I started a career in custom wood-working, exchanging my time for money to pay my family's growing bills. During that stage in my life, a co-worker introduced me to a Network Marketing business... and it changed my life. I put a lot of time and dedication into that business and at the age of 23, I hit the second highest position in the company. I accomplished this in just six months! That is when I decided to go full-time, and I have been a full-time Network Marketer ever since.

In August of 2007, one of my good friends introduced me to a Network Marketing company in the health and wellness industry. I was open-minded, although a bit skeptical... but I had to see what she was doing. I looked at the company overview and immediately got excited. Our society had become much more health conscious, and that strengthened my belief that the Health & Wellness

Industry was going to be the next Trillion Dollar industry. I know one thing in business: it's being in the right place at the right time. This company was at that point. I had to make a move.

Thanks to that decision; I now live an amazing lifestyle with so much flexibility and freedom. Better yet, I have helped thousands of people walk away from their jobs and experience that same lifestyle. I have so much pride in myself and my time, especially since at the time of this writing, I have over 25 millionaires in my organization!

Improving your health and allowing you to live a free lifestyle while helping others; that's what Network Marketing does.

That's what it did for me.

# MY FIRST 90 DAYS

My first 90 days in Network Marketing was different from my second 90 days. During my first 90 days, I was still working in construction. I wanted to get out of that job. I was in that company for a while and it was very crazy and super stressful... and then I was in a car accident. I hit rock bottom and lost everything in that company... and I was back to square one. The second time around, I knew that I had to do everything right so that wouldn't happen again. You hear so many stories from top producers and top leaders in the industry about what they did to be successful. I had to stop putting the key in the electrical socket, so to say. I had to learn and be coachable. It was kind of like when you restart your computer - it runs a lot better.

I thought of my second 90 days as a second chance, and it was also my last chance. I didn't even have enough money to join the company. I didn't even tell my friend who introduced me to the company that I didn't have enough money. I just crossed my fingers and went into overdraft. It's funny, I was worse off the second time around than when I had started the first time at 23 years old. I had to move back to my mom's house and borrow her car to do my business. Of course I didn't tell anybody.

I was doing meetings at Starbucks, telling people that we were gonna be successful, that this is THE company, telling them how ground floor it was. All while my phone was ringing off the hook, my mom wanted her car back. One time, I walked out of a meeting to answer the phone, and it was my mom yelling at me that she needed to go to the store and I needed to get her car back, now. Think about that; here I am, painting a vision to someone about the future of this business, how we were gonna be successful, how we were gonna be millionaires... I came back from the phone call to tell them I have another business appointment... talk about mindset!

I made some money the first couple of weeks in the business and rented a car for 30 days. Well, I told them I was renting it for a week. I was doing meetings, driving around from Los Angeles to San Diego and San Jose, all over Southern California. I got a call from the rental company telling me that I needed to bring the car back. I told them that I still needed the car and asked them to just keep charging me! I needed the car! Eventually they made me bring the car back, so I swapped the car out for another rental so I could continue working my business. That was my first month in the business.

Fast forward to 90 days in this business and I now had two cars; a car from the company and my own brand new $100,000 Jaguar which I parked at my brand new 5 bedroom house. That's right; I went from living with my mom and borrowing cars, to having two cars and a huge house in 90 days. I don't say this to impress you, I say this to impress upon you the need for massive action in your first 90 days in Network Marketing. I was all in. I drove those rental cars around telling people either you're part of the business or you're part of the pavement, get out of my way! It's amazing because in those 90 days, not too many people told me NO. That's because they could see where I was going, and that I was all in. That's important; if people know that you know where you are going, they will be afraid not to follow you.

If you don't know where you're going, if you don't have the mindset, no one will follow you.

# PRODUCTS VS SERVICES

I've been in Network Marketing for 15 years as of December 2015. This is what I have done most of my adult life. The first business that I was involved in was a telecom service business. It was a business where we weren't really selling anything, we were switching people's services over for them. It was very easy in the beginning since we had the best rate in town for long distance - this was way back when long distance calling was very expensive. But it got real complicated when we began to do local service, and as the years progressed, VOIP became very popular and became a way cheaper alternative. What I noticed when we were building the business was that people weren't keeping up with the tech-savviness of everything. So things like resetting routers and plugging VOIP into the TV and whatnot were too difficult for people to understand. That greatly slowed down the duplication process, and in Network Marketing, you need to duplicate yourself out as many times as you can. When you have a service that's a little complicated, it creates a bottleneck. Some businesses out there require that you get a license to sell the service. When you think about that, people are busy. They work all week and don't have the time or even WANT to have to get a license; people like to keep it simple.

Being in the service industry for so long, I was conditioned that I didn't want anything to do with lotions and potions. I thought, "No way, I'm not having a garage full of this stuff, and driving around town selling this stuff." But after some research, I found out that the product industry is what made up Network Marketing. It's what started this whole industry! It was the most simple and duplicatable business out there because it was tangible. A housewife could easily share the product with someone. Larry the construction worker, Joe the entrepreneur, Grandma Sue... All could share a product and refer a customer. It was simple. And believe me, I don't knock services or products, you can make money in Network Marketing with either one. But what I found out about the product industry is that the profit margins are so much higher than the service industry, which leads to having higher residual incomes. In services, you are the middleman and are getting a little commission paid out to you. But with products having higher margins, the company pays out more to the compensation plan.

What was most interesting to me about the service industry is that while I worked with those companies, I never had anybody call me emotional about how much money they saved on their phone bill and how they now can send their kids to college. But in the product industry, my leaders and I get calls all the time from people crying happy tears. Pain going away, helping with arthritis, and how their mom can feel her feet again. At first I didn't think this was for real, but when I saw the products working on my own family and myself, I knew this was powerful. And once you share a product with someone and it changes their life, they will never get off the product. You have a life-long customer. And once a family member finds out that you've helped another family member of theirs by providing them with a product that made them feel better, you don't even need to promote that product, it has promoted itself for you. I've seen people that were just product users come into the business and become $15,000+ a month earners because they believed in the product so much. That's the biggest difference between services and products but like I said, you can make money with both, I just prefer products!

# Chapter 2

# WHY

Your why is so important. Your why will change, and change depending on where you are in life. In this business, we say if your why doesn't make you cry, it's not big enough. It's GOTTA make you cry, you gotta shed a tear when you think about it. I would run through walls for my why. I would wake up in the morning with a fire inside of me for my why. That's what will drive you every day. Because there are gonna be some negative people out there (i.e.; haters). Your why has to be able to drive you through that. Take that negativity and use it as fuel to accomplish your why. That's exactly what I did. I took in all the negativity from family, coworkers, friends, and all people that thought this wasn't going to work, and I fueled the fire. And boy did it pay off. Those people that were negative before are not negative anymore - that's for sure. The best thing you can do to really see what your why is is to sit down and ask yourself questions until you start tearing up. "Why am I doing this business? Why do I want to have a lot of money? I want to send my kids to the best colleges..." That last one was definitely part of my why. Keep asking yourself why you want the thing you're thinking about and when your eyes get teary and your voice gets quivery, you've got it.

Also, make a Dream Board. A Dream Board is a tangible representation of achieving a large scale goal. Take a picture of your family and put that picture in a vacation you want to go on. Put it in front of the house you want to live in. Go drive by the house you want and take a picture of it. Go drive the car of your dreams and take a picture of yourself in it. With technology nowadays, you can create your Dream Board while on the road! Ferrari selfies anyone? Put yourself in the situation you want to be in and dream. I do it all the time. I still do it to this day. It's ok to dream - just write it down. Put your family in it. That is your Dream Board. Then you can begin to fulfill it. When you fulfill you Dream Board, make a new one! Envision it every day, and your dream will come true. They did for me.

# MY WHY

My why is different now than it was when I first started. When I first started in Network Marketing back in December of 2000, my why was to get out of my job. I was 23 years old, I was in construction, and just wanted to get the heck out of there. I had my son at 16, and I wanted to give him a better quality of life, and I wanted to make more money. I worked my butt off at that job but I didn't have the lifestyle I wanted. I wanted to live "the lifestyle." Drive nice cars, wear nice suits and just not get dirty every day like I did in construction. That was my why in the beginning. I saw what the potential, the magnitude of what Network Marketing could do for me. First I saw getting out of a job, being able to work from home. Then I saw that I could become a multi-millionaire, help my family out. And then I saw that I could help others do the same thing. That's what got me excited about this industry. Since I didn't have my high school diploma, I didn't have many options. This was perfect for me. Network Marketing didn't care what your education was, what your background was, what your race was. It didn't matter. What mattered was hard work, dedication and motivation. With that, you can become successful.

As I grew in the business and got older, things started to change and my why became a little different. In my first company, things started happening, politics, and things weren't going my way and I started losing everything. And then I got in a car accident and couldn't work for about 6 months, so I really lost everything up to that point. Here I was, even though I had quit my job and gone full time in Network Marketing, I lost everything I worked for. When my friend called me about a health and wellness industry, I was totally negative. I was already in a service company and I never wanted to sell lotions or potions, but I respected my friend. She was very successful so I took a look at the business, and there I was, starting all over again and redeveloping my WHY. My new why was to get back above water, get out of debt, fix my credit, pay off my taxes.

Six years later, my WHY changed again. I met my wife and now had 2 daughters and my son. I wanted to give THEM the best life I could. I wanted my kids to have the best schooling. I wanted to give my wife her dream wedding. My parents had been struggling, and automatically I wanted to help them. My dad worked his whole life and my mom was a stay-at-home mom. I wanted to help ALL my family.

So remember, your why needs to be the driving force in your business. If you've done a business like this and quit, it's because you didn't have a big enough fire underneath you to keep you going. Your why is the reason to do that meeting, to get on that call, to get to the international event 4,000 miles away. It's ok if your WHY changes from time to time, just know that it has to be there to guide you through all the NOs, the rejection, the politics, the corporate compensation plan changes, the times you website is down... My why has gotten me through that and then some, that's how powerful it is.

*If your why doesn't make you cry,*

*it's not big enough.*

# YOUR STORY

Your WHY and your current situation create your story. Your story alone could be the main reason people get involved in your business. In most parts of life, but especially in Network Marketing, stories sell. You could spend an hour with someone explaining to them how awesome your compensation plan is or how great your product tastes but they'll end up saying no because they can't relate to it.

Stories create a relationship between you and your prospects, and then you and your team. I've heard many members of my team tell my story about getting kicked out of high school and how now I make millions teaching others to become millionaires. It motivates people to know that "Hey, my upline did it, why can't I?" My company created a video about me showing my story and how Network Marketing has changed my life and it has thousands of views.

Now, your story doesn't stay the same forever, one day you're gonna add "and then I became a millionaire" to it. I have many different ways I tell my story depending on what group of people I am presenting it to, but the core remains the same. And that's what you need to establish. If I found you on the street and asked you, "What's your story?" would you have something ready to go? Could you keep me engaged? Write down you story and learn how to present it to someone in one minute.

Of course, if your story doesn't involve explosions or flying a jet, that doesn't mean it isn't a great story! Let's say you're a single mom raising two kids... That right there is a great story! Use your hardship, your obstacles, the negativity in your life, use it all to develop a story. You never know when someone is sitting in a room going through the same things that you are.

*Use the following dream planner as a starting point for your dream board. Fill in the areas with what dream you want to achieve for yourself and your family. When you are done, make sure to make a big version with pictures and put it in an area of your home with lots of traffic so you can look at it every day!*

# DREAM BOARD PLANNER

Write down a dream you have relating to the topic in the box. Remember to make a large one later with pictures! (ie; a picture of a Ferrari under **fun**)

| business | wealth |
|---|---|
|  |  |
| self-care | family and friends |
|  |  |
| fun | major scary goals |
|  |  |

# Chapter 3

# GOALS

Goals are something you want to achieve. Short term, long term, and super long term. A goal fuels your WHY. A goal is something like, "I want to hit a rank," or "I want to be a Regional Vice President." Goal setting is so important. The most successful people in the world set goals. If you don't have a target, you're not gonna hit anything! Anything small or large can be a goal. Set a goal like I want to hit this rank/position on this day. I want my team to be "this" big or my volume to be "this" big by this day. Your goal can be to become full time in your company; that's huge! You WANT to be full time in this business. If you have a car program, get that car! Because people are watching you, and you keep hitting those goals, it's more success for you to show others. There are people that will join your business as soon as they see you hit those goals. They are literally waiting for you to get that car, to reach that rank. That is why goals are so important. Write them down so you can look at them every day. I know some people that write down their goals and tape them near their bed so that that's the first thing they see every day. If you are married or have kids, set goals WITH your family. If you think you are involved in this business on your own, you don't have to be. Your family is involved because you are out doing meetings and sacrificing your time with them for your business. What I tell my leaders is set your goals with your kids/family. Say, "Look kids, when I hit this rank, we're going to Disneyland. We're gonna go for days and you can do whatever you want." This way, you have the whole family keeping you accountable. It's one thing to be accountable to your upline, but it's another to be accountable to a 5 year old that tells you "When are you gonna be a Diamond? I wanna go to Disneyland!" It's the best accountability in the world! I highly advise to do this. Set your goals and hit them. Just make sure to not set outlandish goals. Set realistic goals. If you set a goal that is so farfetched that you don't hit it, you'll want to give up in your first week! If your goals are reasonable but you fall short, you just gotta adjust your goals a little bit. And if you hit your goal, double it or otherwise make a bigger goal! I do that! I have goals I make but then have to adjust them. The important thing is to set those goals.

*Use the following Goal Setting Worksheet to help
plan out some goals for yourself!
WHAT is the goal you want to reach and HOW are
you going to reach it?*

|  | WHAT? | HOW? | WHEN? |
|---|---|---|---|
| **DAILY GOALS** |  |  |  |

|  | WHAT? | HOW? | WHEN? |
|---|---|---|---|
| **WEEKLY GOALS** |  |  |  |

|  | WHAT? | HOW? | WHEN? |
|---|---|---|---|
| **MONTHLY GOALS** |  |  |  |

|  | WHAT? | HOW? | WHEN? |
|---|---|---|---|
| YEARLY GOALS |  |  |  |

|  | WHAT? | HOW? | WHEN? |
|---|---|---|---|
| PERSONAL GOALS |  |  |  |

|  | WHAT? | HOW? | WHEN? |
|---|---|---|---|
| FAMILY GOALS |  |  |  |

# Chapter Summary

- A goal is something you want to achieve.
- Because people are watching you, and you keep hitting those goals, it's more success for you to show others.
- There are people that will join your business as soon as you hit those goals, they are literally waiting for you.
- Set goals with your family to maximize motivation (a kid will remind you to hit the next rank EVERY DAY.)
- If you set a goal that is so farfetched that you don't hit it, you'll give up your first week.
- Set realistic goals!

# Chapter 4

# MINDSET

When you get involved in this business, your mindset has to be 100% coachable. The upline has a system and knows the business and knows exactly what you are going to go through. They know how your family is going to be, how your friends are going to react, and basically everything that you are going to go through in your first 90 days. They know and I know, it isn't any different to what we already went through. Be coachable, because that will guide you to having the right mindset.

In this business, you have to have long-term thinking. This is not a get-rich-quick scheme. This business is called netWORK marketing for a reason! Yes, your upline has a system that they know will work if duplicated out to the team... but there's no way around working the business... YOU gotta do it! Some people may reach success faster than others, but you have to have a long-term mindset because this business is an emotional rollercoaster. You WILL have good days and you

WILL have bad days. You'll have positive people and you'll have negative people. Of course you will! This is life!

When you first get involved in your business, you're pumped up and excited! You just got out of a home meeting or business opportunity and you're feeling great. You're driving home and you call your mom up and say, "Hey mom, you're gonna be my first customer." Then she says, "What are you, crazy? What are you getting involved in? Get your money back, I don't want anything to do with this!" And you think, "Wait a minute, if my mom won't be my customer, then no one will be my customer! My mom would do anything for me, this is crazy!" So you call your upline and say, "I don't know if I made the right decision getting involved in this, my mom won't be my customer!" And there's the emotional rollercoaster. Now you're down. Then your upline tells you, "We'll have a home meeting for you and we'll get people signed up." Now you're excited! And you call up 30 people and they tell you they are coming for sure! So now comes your home meeting, it's 7:30 on a Tuesday night and you and your upline are ready at your house... and no one shows up. Now you're going crazy, calling people and no one is answering your call! You say, "Man, I don't know if this business is right for me." Your upline says, "It's ok, we'll schedule another meeting, don't worry about it." Your upline leaves... and then your phone rings. It's one of your prospects. "Hey buddy, I'm so sorry but we were caravanning together and one of us got a flat tire so we all had to pull over. But hey, we don't need to see your presentation, we'll do your business. We even got the tow truck guy to do it." You were so down in the dumps and now you're amped up out of your mind! So all those people joined your business, and then a week later, everyone goes in the Witness Protection Program or something, because all of a sudden you can't get hold of ANYONE. And now you're down in the dumps again. Up and down and up and down. The best advice I can give to you is stay level-minded. Don't go too high and don't go too low on this rollercoaster. And remember, you aren't selling to people to do the business. You're sorting. Amateurs sell in this business, professionals sort through people.

When you talk to people, you're gonna find three types of people: positive people, skeptical people, and negative people. We don't prejudge people. We share the business, share the opportunity, and they will decide who they are. Your mindset should be to go out there and share with EVERYBODY and see what kind of person each one will be.

Have long-term thinking, be coachable, and understand that your upline can help you avoid a lot of those things that you are going to go through in the beginning that are kind of frustrating, BUT you gotta listen. If you are like me my first time around and you gotta stick the key in the electrical socket, take my advice: keep it easy and listen to your upline because they will keep you level headed.

When I first started, I was a little more hardcore. I was growing up in a really tough environment so in my head, this was it. This business was IT. When people were negative, I thought they were crazy! When I got negative responses and people told me no, I would actually get offended. I didn't understand! What's wrong with these people? This is the best opportunity in the world! What I didn't understand was that it was them, not me. So in the beginning, my mindset was, "I'm gonna make this happen with or without anyone. If my family and friends don't want to do this, I'm gonna find strangers that will." If it's gonna be, it's up to me.

That was my mentality. The key to this business is having that strong mindset.

# Chapter Summary

- Be coachable.
- This is not a get-rich-quick scheme.
- Set long-term goals for a long-term business.
- Stay level-minded.
- Amateurs sell, professionals sort.
- 3 Types of People: Positive people, skeptical people and negative people.
- Don't pre-judge.

# Chapter 5

# PROSPECT LIST

When you first get started in the business, you want to make a list of 100 names and numbers. Your list should consist of friends, family, coworkers, acquaintances, distant relatives, anyone you can think of. Even if you don't have their phone numbers, just write their names down and you can get their numbers later. The reason you want to make this list is because you want to be able to check people off the list. And remember that your list is gold. Your list is everything you need to build your business, because you never know who this business is for and not for.

Once you make your list, you can start sorting through it. When you start contacting people you're gonna get three types of people. You're gonna get red apples, green apples, and rotten apples.

Red apples are positive people. They're the kind of people that you will call and say, "Hey, I'm having a meeting this Tuesday at 7:30 and I'd like for you to come,"and they will respond, "I'll be there. Can I bring somebody? Do you need anything?" Red apples are no problem, they are there.

And then there's gonna be green apples – people that are going to ask you questions. When you call them, they're gonna say, "What is this?" It's kind of like if you ask someone to go to the movies with you and they say, "What movie are we gonna watch? Who wrote the movie? Who produced it? Who's driving?" And you're like, what the heck? All I did was ask you if you wanted to go see a movie and you're drilling me with all these questions. There's just people out there like that. They want to know how much you know. Those green apples will turn either rotten or red, depending on your response.

Then there's rotten apples. Now there's two types of rotten apples on the list. There's the okays and not-okays. The first kind of rotten apple will say, "Look man, I see what you're doing. I'm not interested. I'm good where I am. I'm okay in life. But I wish you the best of luck." And I respect people like that. But then there's the not-okay rotten apples. The really negative people. We all know really negative people. They'll try to rain on your parade. They'll try to knock you out the box. You'll call them up and they'll say, "Oh my god, you got into one of those things. I can't believe you." And they'll go around telling everybody what you're doing. And what I find amazing about that is that most of the time it's the brokest people we know that do this. Here you are trying to do something with your life, trying to become successful. And they have no solutions to help your family out, or themselves, or anybody else... but they'll try to knock you down. They say that misery loves company, but misery also hates to lose company. Remember if you buy someone's opinion, you're gonna buy their lifestyle. Be careful who you're listening to. When you come across a negative person on your list, just let them be. Change the subject. It's not worth it. Remember: amateurs sell, professionals sort. We're sorting through your list to find the people that want to make it happen.

Another important reason why you want to make your list as big as you can is that your list is somebody else's list. You're not the only person that knows these people. Other people know your people too. You don't want to know how many times I've been to a presentation where two different people knew the same prospect in the room. And one will say to the other, "what are you doing here?" And they'll say, "oh, so-and-so invited me. Aw man, I was gonna call you." Their face looked like they saw a ghost when they saw that person there. And all of a sudden that prospect signs up and becomes successful... and now you have to see them at every event. That was your dentist, or your doctor, or your neighbor, and you didn't call them. So somebody else put them on their list, and they called them.

Never prejudge anybody. Don't think people are too successful to do this business, or not successful enough. And remember that your prospects are in all different categories of life. There's people out there that make a lot of money in life but have no time (and honestly, what's the use of making all this money if you have no time?) Then there's people out there that have a lot of time and no money. And there's people that have no time and no money. What I'm trying to say is that people get involved in this business for different reasons - that is why you want to offer this business to everyone, This is important: don't push it away from them, let them push it away.

So, make that list, make it as big as you can, with a minimum of 100 names. They say that the average 21 year old kid knows 2000 people by first name. If you make a list, actually write it down - not on your cell phone or your computer, write it down – this list is your success. The bigger the list, the bigger success you will have.

It's funny because I only put like fifteen people on my first list, and it was the people I was most comfortable with. I knew them, they would do the business because I told them to do it. Here I was, sticking the key in the electrical socket again. That's why we tell you to be coachable. I needed to make a bigger list. Fifteen people is nothing. I call those fifteen people, and then what? But after I actually sat down and really focused on making a list, I easily made a list of 200-300 people. I didn't have anybody's numbers, I got that stuff later. I even wrote down my parents' friends, my dad's coworkers – I knew them and they knew me. That's what your list should consist of. I started really thinking outside the box and really expanded my list. What's amazing is that some of the people who knew me the least were the most open-minded people, and just saw the business and immediately got started and had success. And some of the people that were really close to me that I thought would be perfect for this business didn't even get started. So you never know. The ones you think will, won't. And the ones you think won't, will. I never understood that until I made that big list.

# Chapter Summary

- Make a list of 100 names and numbers.
- Know the three types of people: red apples, green apples, and rotten apples.
- When you come across a negative person on your list, just let them be. Change the subject. It's not worth it.
- Your list is somebody else's list too.
- Don't think people are too successful to do this business, or not successful enough.
- Don't push it away from them, let them push it away.
- The bigger the list, the bigger success you will have.
- The ones you think will, won't and the ones you think won't, will.

# Chapter 6

# EDIFICATION

I really didn't understand how powerful edification was when I first started. Growing up in my environment, when you would talk good about someone it kind of showed weakness. So it was very different for me to talk someone up, build someone up. And especially, me being in the construction world at the time, which is a negative environment, we never talked up about anyone. So I didn't really understand this idea. Once I understood edification and how powerful it was, it would empower my upline and my team into action. It was like an "a-ha" moment. It was amazing.

Of course, you don't lie. You just build up, talk good about your upline. Don't say things like, "this is my friend" because they're not gonna show up as your friend, with a hat on, jeans, cut-off shorts. They come as your business partner. They come as if they've been edified. Once I edified my upline, to a degree where they were empowering to my team, this was an easy business. It was EASY.

You can definitely tell when you've been edified by how the prospect reacts when they meet you or greet you on the phone. The more you edify and respect your upline, the more your prospect will do for you. It's not for your upline's ego. It's so they can move the prospect into action. You can't tell somebody, "My buddy Angel is gonna roll over and do a presentation for you." And your buddy Angel rolls over in baggy jeans, a t-shirt, and a hat on. What are your prospects going to think? Let's say you said, "Listen, I have one of the top executives in the world coming here to my house to show you the business, you really need to hear whats going on." And your upline shows up dressed as a top money earner ready to deliver the goods. By doing this, you build the credibility up about your upline which will make him/her more effective with your prospects.

*Here are a few sample scripts for edifying your sponsor or upline leader... If your upline has a specific script, please use that as that is what works in your organization! Replace the underlined areas to reflect your company's ranks.*

**NEW LEADER (LOW-MID TO MID RANK)**

"This individual has been promoted to one of the first positions in the company, by following our system that ensures success. We are so fortunate to have them here to teach us how we can do the same thing.

Let me introduce Mr./ Mrs. _____ "

**MID RANK LEADER**

"Not only has this individual been successful, by promoting to the *# of MID RANK POSITION, ex '3rd'* earned position in the company, but they have mentored and assisted others in succeeding as well. Part-time, they are able to make what most of us earn in our full time careers!

Let me introduce *RANK* Mr./Mrs. _____ who will teach us how we can do the same."

**MID-HIGH TO HIGH RANK LEADER**

"This individual is a leader's leader! They have earned a position within *YOUR COMPANY* where their income parallels monthly what most people make in year. They have stepped up within the compensation plan and are mentoring others to succeed within our System! They are here to teach us how we can have options and choices financially, because they are living examples of how *YOUR COMPANY* works, please let me introduce

*RANK* Mr./Mrs. _____."

**VERY HIGH RANK LEADER**

"The individual we are privileged to hear from today has EARNED the Top position with *YOUR COMPANY*! *RANK*s have been documented to be in the of 1% of highest-paid earners in the World. They are hand picked to expand and develop the next wave of leaders and teams nationally and internationally with *YOUR COMPANY*. With organizations as large as theirs, we are lucky to have some time with their experience and knowledge to teach us all that *YOUR COMPANY* has to offer. Please let me introduce *RANK* Mr./Mrs._____

# Chapter Summary

- The more you edify and respect your upline, the more your prospect will.
- Edification is something we may be uncomfortable with but once you learn to do it properly, this business becomes easy.
- If you're no good at it, learn scripts.
- Your upline will be more effective with your prospects once properly edified.

# Chapter 7

# INVITING

When you're inviting people to a presentation, you want to keep it simple. We say, "Don't firehose people." If someone is thirsty, you want to give them a glass of water, not spray them with a fire hose. You don't want to give them too much information because people will try to make a decision based on what you tell them. They will take their past experiences and whatever misconceptions they may have about what they think your business is, based on whatever information you give them. Your leaders and upline have developed scripts for whatever product or service your company distributes, so use them!

K.I.S.S - Keep it Super Simple. My team keeps it very simple, we lean on the relationship. We tell our new distributors to ask their prospects to come over to support their business, to take a look at it. Let them know that it may or may not be for them, take the opportunity away from them a little. If the prospect is a friend or family member, why wouldn't they come support you? I would support any of my friends or family that asked me this way, I don't care what business it is. If you were opening up a restaurant or a retail store, your friends would come to the grand opening to support you. This is the same thing! So remember to keep it super simple, lean on the relationship, and don't give too much information! This way, your prospects come to support you and your new business and you can pack the room! Remember to know your role. When you first get started in the business, you are the inviter. You pique someone's interest and then you pass to the upline and let them present the information.

*Use the following sample script for inviting people to your event. If your upline has a specific script, please use it as that is what works in your organization! Replace the underlined areas to reflect your company/industry.*

## SAMPLE SCRIPT FOR INVITING

Event Date _____

Event Time_____

Hello _____ do you have a few minutes?

*(Wait for response)*

What are you doing _____ at _____?

*(Response)*

Great! The reason I am asking is because I'm Excited about a ground floor opportunity and I'm having a few key people over to my house to see what's going on. Can I count on you to be there?

If they ask questions:

I can't explain it over the phone but I can tell you this, its Ground Floor, it deals with the _____ industry. Plus the Executive coming can answer all of your questions. Right now all I want to know is if you will be there to support me.

If they persist on knowing more, connect them with an expert on a three-way call or send them to a video with a quick overview of your company.

YOU ARE NEW, and don't want to confuse them.

# Types of People

RED APPLES:       Positive People
GREEN APPLES:    People with Questions
ROTTEN APPLES: Negative People

REMEMBER THE **SW** RULE:
**S**ome **W**ill,
**S**ome **W**on't,
**S**ome **W**ait,
**S**o **W**hat...
NEXT!!!!!!!!

# Chapter Summary

- Keep it simple.
- Don't "firehose" people.
- People will make a decision based on what you tell them.
- Learn your team scripts.
- Lean on the relationship.
- Let them know that it may or may not be for them (fear of loss).
- When you first get started in the business, you are the inviter.
- **SW** Rule!

# Chapter 8

# PRESENTING

Your job as a new distributor is to invite people to the event. Whether it's a home meeting, a two on one, a hotel meeting, webinar, conference call, regional event, or huge amphitheater event, the expert that you invite will present the opportunity. This could be your upline or other invited guest; basically the expert is anybody but yourself since you are new to the business. When you invite your warm market, these are people that know you, therefore they won't listen to you. Let the expert present the business. After the presentation, the people that saw it will either: become a business partner, become a customer, or tell you it's not for them. Your job is to help identify where the prospect is leaning towards and have them speak to an expert (could be another person in the business at your meeting). Have the expert close them for you as a partner or customer. I see so many people think that if the person doesn't sign up in their business, they've lost them. Get them as a customer! Turn all NOs into a YES. Get that person in some other way, especially if you are in a product company with a solid product. The NO to the business could be a YES to the product and that person can become a "customer getter." We have people in our organization that became very successful distributors who started out as very happy customers. This is essentially what a presentation is for, identifying and sorting between your prospects to find out if someone is going to be a business partner or a customer.

People only retain about 10% of what they hear and there are 3 things that they will ask themselves at a presentation:

*Can I do this?*

*Does this work?*

*Do I trust the person who invited me here?*

If your overall presentation answers those three questions, that person is going to be your business partner. Why wouldn't they?

# COMMON
# OBJECTIONS AND ANSWERS

**I have no money!**
- If money wasn't the issue, what would your thoughts be on moving forward?
- What if it were free, what would happen?
- What's your understanding of how you make your money back?

**I need more information!**
- What would you like to know?
- If I can get you the info you're looking for, then what?

**It's not for me!**
- What's not for you?
- Why's that?
- What don't you like about the business?
- No Problem. How come?

**I'm too busy!**
- What if you weren't too busy?
- What if you had time and money?
- What if partnering with us gave you the free time to do what you really want?
- What if we can work around your schedule, what then?

## Is this a pyramid?

- No those are illegal. What do you know about the differences between network marketing vs a pyramid?
- Define pyramid?
- Show the diagram of corporate structure vs. Net work Marketing

## I'm not a sales man/woman?

- What if being a sales person wasn't needed to be successful in this business?
- What if I told you that most of the Leaders never had sales experience?

## I have to talk to my spouse first!

- Why's that?
- If he/she had said "yes," what would you do?

## My job won't let me do other stuff!

- What if there was a way around this issue. How open are you?
- If they said it was okay, what would you do?

# Chapter Summary

- The expert is anyone in the business but yourself.
- Your job is to invite people to the event.
- After the presentation, identify where the prospect is leaning (customer or distributor).
- Turn all NOs in to a YES (don't leave money on the table).
- Some very successful distributors started out as very happy customers.
- Remember, people will ask themselves three questions:

  - *Can I do this?*

  - *Does this work?*

  - *Do I trust the person who invited me here?*

# Chapter 9

# PROMOTING

You're always promoting. You promote the next conference call, business opportunity meeting, a Super Saturday, regional event, national event, international event... whatever the event is. You're always promoting the next event. I've seen people in this industry who were the worst presenters and worst inviters BUT they were the best promoters. They would bring so many people to the events and became so good at promoting that the events built their business. Get good at promoting events. You want to be the Don King of promoting your business' events. Go out there and promote the next event like it's the last event there ever will be.

Yes, technology can help connect people online no matter where you are in the world but NOTHING beats a face to face interaction. Events make money. Once someone attends an event, the most important thing that will happen is their belief level will change. Events will have a huge impact on the long-term success of any organization, especially if it's an event that people have to travel to. Anyone who tries to tell you that they can have the same effect holding a webinar for 200 people as they would holding a meeting for 200 people in Las Vegas, is not a top earner in Network Marketing. But even from small events like a PBR or Opportunity Call, you gain strength and willpower.

At events, the top earners and leaders will say one thing that clicks with you and ignites a fire inside of you. I've had hundreds of those moments from events and let me tell you, I owe my current life to them. They are that powerful. What I'm talking about is "social proof." All of us are wired to seek proof from places other than from ourselves. If you're at a Business Opportunity Meeting and the presenter says "Everyone who is in the business, could you please stand up," you see lots of other people who've made the same decision that you did to join your business, and to you that feels good. I've even had some of my team members say to me "Next event, I'm gonna be at least a [top rank] because I'm tired of having to wait in line with everyone else." You should have seen the fire inside them!

When your belief level goes up, your action level goes up. When your action level goes up, your results go up. If you look at this following a 1 to 10 scale (10 being the highest), let's say your belief level before the event was a 5. If your belief level is at a 5, your action level will be around 4 to 5. What would your results level be at? Probably a 4 or 5. But if you go to an event and your belief goes to a 10, what is your action level going to be? Probably a 9 or 10. What are your results going to be? 9 or 10. This is why events and promoting those events are so important: because without belief, you are not going to be successful. You need the validation and conviction from the event, and your team does too, along with the training and everything else that goes along with it. You can't get this from sitting at home. Get yourself and your team always promoting and attending the next event.

The first step in developing a promoting culture in your team is to be more committed than anyone else. That means you have to lead by example and NEVER miss an event. They say that at each event, half of the people in the room won't be at the NEXT event. But the half that was there will end up, on average, making double the income of those who were not. And at the next event, same thing, half will be at the NEXT NEXT event and half will not. But those who keep coming back, on average, double their earnings compared to the rest of the people in the room. Based on this, if you keep coming back to each event, eventually you'll be among the top earners in the room.

If I told you that I'd give you $1,000 for every person that you brought to an event... how many people would you have there? That's how you have to promote events - like there's a big bonus coming to you the more people you have there. And really there is, because your team will be more dedicated and their belief level will be so high that they'll commit themselves to being promoters!

# Chapter Summary

- You're always promoting the next event.
- Events make money.
- People don't know what they don't know.
- Events make the belief level go up.
- Events will have a huge impact on your long-term.
- Events allow new people to see others having success: If they can do it, I can do it.
- When belief level goes up, action level goes up.
- Be more committed than anyone else.

# Chapter 10

# RECRUITING

If you want a bigger organization, bigger volume, or bigger checks, you have to recruit people. Nothing is gonna happen in your business if you don't do it! A lot of people get scared at the word "recruiting" but you have to understand that the best companies recruit the best talent to come work for their organization. What do the biggest sports teams in the world do? They recruit the best athletes so their team becomes the best. That's exactly what you wanna do in Network Marketing. Go out there and find somebody that is better than you. I've had people tell me, "Well, I don't know a lot of people." Well, go find someone who knows a lot of people! I've also gotten, "I don't like talking to people." Hmm, how would I respond to this... Oh yeah! "Well go find people who like to talk to people!"

You cannot run your business by saying "I got into this business and I think it might work. I'm not sure but it sounds good!" People will not follow you if you don't know where you're going. If you know where you are going, people will be afraid NOT to follow you! People go out and work that grind every week. They go to work where they have a mutual relationship with their boss; they don't like their boss and their boss doesn't like them. But they have to deal with it because they gotta pay the bills. Next time you stop at a red light during the week when people are getting off of work, look around to the other drivers. Look to see who is excited. No one's excited! Everyone just wants to honk at you and tell you to get out of their way. Well, at least that's how it is in Los Angeles. If you are excited, that means you're different. If you are different from most people by being excited, people are going to gravitate towards you and want to know "Why are you excited? What do you know that I don't know?" And guess what? Your business is the answer.

I duplicate out to my distributors and teach that when you are making your lists, you categorize your prospects as reds, greens, and blues. Reds are people that you look up to, people that have influence. Greens are people on the same level as you, your peers. And blues are people that look up to you. People will always try to choose the path of least resistance. They'll go after their Blues. Why? Because Blues will listen to them! "Hey Cousin Jason, get to my house ASAP" and he comes over right away. If you run a business and have employees, you'll go after your employees. Why? Because Blues will listen to you. Why is this a problem? Because remember, in Network Marketing, everything that you do will duplicate out to your team, whether it's good or bad. If you recruit a Blue, your Blue will recruit their Blues. Somewhere down the line, you'll be presenting the business to a 14 year old who is trying to use their mom's social security number to get into the business (believe me, it's happened). And then the Blue team you built dies out. But if you go out there and recruit the owner of the company you work for or your uncle who is a doctor, you will get a different result.

Ask yourself this question right now, If you were to start a traditional business, who would be on your Board of Directors? Your cousin Jason who still lives at home or your uncle who is a Doctor? Those people are the exact same people you want as your top business partners in your Network Marketing business! After developing a solid system and perfecting it, I found out the following statistics:

1 Red is equivalent to 30 Greens and 100 Blues. Is a Red difficult to get into your business? Probably. But get one Red excited about your opportunity, and you'll start living the most exciting part of your business!

## KEY TRAITS WHEN RECRUITING

- Posture, Confidence, Passion, and Excitement
- Create value and relate to prospects
- Tell stories
- Edify the Presenter
- Sense of Urgency
- Fear of loss
- Know your role

## KEY PHRASES AND QUESTIONS

- If I could show you a way...
- Imagine if you could be at the right place at the right time...
- If the money was right, and could work within your schedule, are you open to an opportunity?
- Are you open to making money outside of what you currently do?
- How much money is "great" money to you?
- How familiar are you with residual income?
- Are you happy with your current level of income? Can you imagine making more?

# Chapter Summary

- Don't let the word recruiting scare you. The best sports teams, biggest corporations, and government all recruit the best of the best.
- People will not follow you if you don't know where you're going.
- Be excited! Excitement creates interest in those around you.
- Reds are people that you look up to, people that have influence.
- Greens are people on the same level as you, your peers.
- Blues are people that look up to you.
- If you were to start a traditional business, who would be on your Board of Directors?

# Chapter 11

# GETTING SOMEONE STARTED

One of the most important things that you should master in your Network Marketing career is getting a new business partner started the right way. The moment that your new team member signs the application, that's when the work begins.

You want to follow the system that your team has developed because that system will be the easiest to duplicate out within your organization. Here is a basic structure of how you should get someone started. If you partner this structure with the system your team is promoting, your team members will be unstoppable, right out the gate.

The key to helping the brand new person is efficiency. You want them to be profitable as soon as possible after joining your team. Let your team member know that you need to set aside at least 45 minutes to an hour of time to sit down with them and get them started. This time needs to be uninterrupted and needs to be done one-on-one, not in a group setting because you may be discussing things they may not want to share in a group setting. This is very important: your new team member deserves this time. They deserve to know the how and why to do the business to maximize their earning potential. If they learn incorrect habits, they will most likely not do well in the business and you will have burned a bridge not only between you and your new team member but between the member and the industry in general.

It is best to have a physical paper that has the starting information that your team promotes. This paper should have basic info like Start Date, 30 Day Date, and a diagram of the first earning position within your company's compensation plan. If that isn't there, draw it and explain it to them! Since not everybody learns things the same way, you are showing them, telling them, and illustrating it to them which should cover most people's learning styles. When your new team member understands the first earning position, they can teach it to others. The goal with duplication and launching a new member is that you want 'teachers teaching teachers.'

Now, here is where it may get emotional. When someone begins a new business venture, they do it for a reason. We covered this in Chapter 2, their WHY. The why is the driving force in that person's business. The emotional rollercoaster of any business, including Network Marketing, can be overcome when there is an internal fire to achieve and make their why come true. Let your new team member take the time to think about why they joined your business and figure out the deep down reason they are doing this... When you see eyes become teary, you've found the why!

Now comes getting some names down on their list. If your team's system has a structure on how to do this, this is is the time when you will show your new member how this is done. Make sure to let them know NOT to pre-judge anybody in their warm market. Also, remind them of people they may not have thought about (their dry cleaner, car wash person, bank teller, their real estate agent, etc.) I always teach this to my team: ask your new person, 'If you were to start a corporation, who would be your board of directors?' and have them put those names down first. This is the best part about Network Marketing as an industry, we get to work with the people we want to work with!

I won't get into too much detail about what scripts you should use or what method of acquiring customers and recruits you should use because this should be outlined in your team's system. What I can recommend is that apart from detailing how to build their team of customers and distributors, emphasize the importance of events. The only way to duplicate yourself out is to lead by example. So if you have a big event coming up, either within your team or your company's corporate events, promote it to the new team member right in the training. Tell them that attending this event is as important as getting other people to this event. If you build the importance and edify the event and the people who will be there, your new team member will too.

The knowledge that you put into your new team member alone is edifying yourself. It isn't about ego, its about building credibility in your team. If they believe you know what to do and where you're going, they will be afraid not to follow you (deja vu?)

After you are done explaining all this to your new team member, make sure to set up their next event where you or one of your leaders will present.

Remember, right OR wrong duplicates down. If you teach the right things, your team will teach the rights things. The same goes for the wrong things. Sometimes, the wrong things duplicates twice as fast so this time spent with a new team member is absolutely critical to your team's success.

# Chapter Summary

- Follow your team's system.
- Be efficient.
- Getting someone started needs to be done one-on-one.
- Your new team member deserves this time.
- Make sure your new team member knows exactly how to be profitable in your company's compensation plan.
- The WHY is the driving force in that person's business.
- Go over the scripts in your system.
- Make sure to highlight the importance of events.
- Right or wrong duplicates down.

# Chapter 12

# FOLLOW UP

The follow up is a very important part of the prospecting process, so you need to give it some thought and time to make sure you get it right. Always remember, you are sorting through people, not selling to them.

When first starting out, it's a good idea to have your upline or mentor helping you with the follow up. If you are meeting someone for the follow up, it wouldn't hurt to bring a more experienced member. This will help boost your effectiveness and make you an expert in no time.

But before you drag your mentor to your next meeting, contact the prospect and let them know you intend to bring someone to the meeting. It would help if you mentioned some of the accomplishments your mentor has in the industry, and encourage the prospect to ask questions. If the follow up is done through a phone call, you can ask them to join in on the three-way call, it works just as well. That process of highlighting your teammates' achievements (edification) helps build respect as your prospect learns more about your team's support system.

You should be very clear that your prospects are not really focused on the fancy products or the awesome compensation plan; what they want is a solution to their problems. This is what you need to target when doing the follow-throughs. At the end of the day, the compensation plan is a vehicle the person will use to solve some of their current problems. When selling a network marketing business, some distributors assume that prospects want in simply because they can make extra money. While the cash might be a good incentive, it is also important to find the solution specific to the prospect. Find out what that extra money could do for the prospect and you have a good place to start from.

Here's a good example of a follow up call:

*"The reason I'm calling you is to ask if you had a chance to check out the information I gave you?"*

If they forgot about it, chances are they want nothing to do with whatever you're doing. If, however they took time to read the material or researched it online after saying they'd think about it, then you can move forward. One of the concepts behind successful follow-ups is to make sure the prospect thinks about the positive aspects of the business opportunity, whether those positive aspects are accurate or they made it up.

By asking the right questions, you can steer the conversation in the right direction and have the prospect focusing on what's important - solving their current problems. Some individuals tend to keep an open mind when faced with new experiences and challenging opportunities and this makes it easier to have them join your organization. Not everyone is built that way and you will come across rigid people who approach business with a narrow focus. Try not to get rattled when your ideas get challenged.

Ideally, you want to get back with your prospect as soon as possible, preferably within a few days, while the idea is still fresh on their minds. You also don't want them to talk to the wrong people and get some negative feedback about the industry. It will be harder to get them past this if the feedback came from close friends or family.

The follow-up process can take anywhere from a few days to several weeks and in some cases, you can go for months or even years building the friendship and the dream, until they are ready to join you. Believe it or not, some people will say NO to you until they see you have some success. When they see you earn a paid vacation or get a company car through your opportunity, then they'll join your business. Your success is your follow up too!

GENERAL TIPS:

- Book the next follow-up at the end of the prospect's first exposure.
- Ideally, you should follow-up within two days.
- You may do the follow-up yourself or have your upline/mentor assist you.
- Start by building a friendship with the prospect. Do this by taking a sincere interest in their dreams, their goals, and their daily life. The stronger the friendship, the stronger the trust and respect you will have for each other.

- Build them a dream. Dreams inspire people and promote action. Find out what their dreams are and what their immediate goals are.
- Train them. Information is very powerful.

# Chapter Summary

- You are sorting through people, not selling to them.
- Have an experienced upline or mentor assist you with the follow up.
- Remember, you're looking for a solution to the prospect's problem.
- Make sure the prospect thinks about the positive aspects of the business opportunity.
- Follow up within a few days maximum.
- Your success is your follow up too!

# Chapter 13

# DUPLICATION

I was fortunate enough to learn from some of the best people in this industry and they kept the system really simple. My mentor was a waiter at a restaurant before getting into Network Marketing. This person kept things simple. Super simple. They taught me that keeping things simple will help you duplicate yourself out faster. You WANT to duplicate yourself out as soon as possible. I remember we had a meeting with about fifteen prospects. My upline was coming out and I was excited because the room was full. But Los Angeles has traffic (weird, huh?) My upline called me and said that they couldn't make it. I freaked out. Not because my upline couldn't show up but because I had to do the presentation myself. I remember writing the presentation on a very sweaty hand and it was all smeared. I could barely read it. I honestly don't know what happened or what I said, but we signed up people that day. What this showed me was that I could do this business, and that what my upline did was duplicate himself out through me.

I just became a clone of him. And then I started doing the same thing to my people. The most important thing was that the system was so simple, it was easy to duplicate out to my team. So when I got into my second Network Marketing company, I knew the importance of developing a simple system that can be duplicated out, a system that anybody could do. So that's what me and my team did. We came up with an A-B-C system for our team to make sure that we could duplicate ourselves out.

A lot of people have a hard time with duplication because they're control freaks and want to do everything. But if you are the one doing all the presentations, all the trainings, everything, all you have is a high-paying job. But once you are able to duplicate yourself out, that's Network Marketing. That's time leverage. That's what we in the industry call beach money because it is true residual income. That is what duplication will do. You want people to have the same presentation on the first level all the way down to the hundredth level. The exact same one. Always ask yourself, "Whatever I'm doing right now, am I being duplicatable?" If you keep it simple, you keep it duplicatable and that is true Network Marketing residual income.

# Chapter Summary

- You WANT to duplicate yourself out as soon as possible.
- If you are the one doing all the presentations, all the trainings, everything, all you have is a high-paying job.
- Don't be a control freak.
- Duplication is the foundation of time leverage.
- The system should be the same all the way down; PBR should be the same on level 1 to level 100.
- Again, KEEP IT SIMPLE!

# Chapter 14

# BOSS MODE

One of the biggest mistakes I see people make in Network Marketing is going into management/boss mode. What a lot of people do is they'll sponsor a couple of business partners and then sit back and wait for them to do something. Umm, no. That isn't going to work. To succeed in Network Marketing, you have to work the numbers. That means that you're in the trenches with your team day in and day out. The cycle of prospecting, presenting the plan, following up, getting customers, and training your team never stops! I do it still on a daily basis not because I need the money, but because I need to lead my team by example. I want to help others achieve what I have, but I need to duplicate myself out to my team and that means leading by example. As your organization gets bigger and you discover leaders that will work the business as hard as you, you can move your focus from doing everything yourself to helping your team work their business. But you shouldn't spend much time managing your team. Maybe when your organization is several hundred people and at least ten to twenty leaders deep, but not when you have just your first few people on your team. People will do what you do. If you sit at home and just try to motivate people by phone, that's what they'll end up doing. However if your team sees you out in the trenches, they'll have no choice but to roll their sleeves up and do what it takes to become successful. My suggestion is never spend more than 20% of your time in boss mode. As your team grows, you may have to spend more time on it - but never spend the majority of your time in boss mode.

Let's say you have a large Opportunity Meeting today. You as the host show up a few hours in advance to make sure everything is set up. A few of your closest distributors show up with you to help make sure everything is set up. You delegate a few tasks to the people who seem to the best for those tasks... and that's it! The rest of your time should be spent prospecting, presenting the plan, closing people, and helping your team follow up with their prospects.

If you begin to be the person that people say "I don't know, ask so-and-so," you're spending too much time in boss mode! Remember, each and every business partner in your organization is in business for themselves. You aren't the CEO of the company, you're their upline. Your tasks are to help your team become a carbon copy of yourself. A lot of network marketers mess this up because they don't spend enough time producing. As a result, they don't build a big team or make money.

I can see why though, boss mode is super easy. You spend all of your time with people who look up to you. You don't get rejection. You get to have fun and not stretch outside of your comfort zone.

Good job boss.

Ask yourself from time to time, "Am I spending too much time in boss mode?" Management activities are ANY activities that don't produce money. Keep saying that in your head and you'll answer your own question very quickly.

Just for your reference and to remind yourself of whether you're acting in Boss Mode or being a true leader, check out the following:

# Boss Mode vs Leader Mode

**In regards to Customer Acquisition...**
- Bosses expect their team to get qualified. They call their team and say things like 'You need 5 customers!' But they haven't got 5 customers themselves.
- Leaders get their customers - They set the pace and work together with their team to get it done.

<br>

- Bosses focus on their own paycheck
- Leaders put their pay checks in their team's hands. They understand that if they help their team get paid, then they will always get paid.

<br>

- Bosses call their downline leaders and have them go get their new rep qualified.
- Leaders do a three-way call to the new rep with their downline leader and schedule a launch/ home meeting AND go to the Home meeting and Launch.

**In regards to Recruiting...**

- Bosses schedule a home meeting with their new reps and tell them to invite a bunch of people, then just show up to the meetings.
- Leaders schedule a home meeting with their new reps and teach them how to get people in front of the business. They role-play contacting and inviting with them, go through their name list, and help them make calls. They even make confirmation calls to ensure a successful meeting.

- When the meeting/PBR is over, bosses leave it up to the host, other reps to close/follow-up.
- Leaders get all the names and numbers of prospects at each meeting and then follow up the next day with the host.

- Bosses look at their team as a downline and a pay check.
- Leaders treat their reps like partners. They create belief in them and use phrases like "we work together," "He is going hit the next rank in the next 30 days!" This gives reps a reputation to live up to.

- Bosses expect their team to bring new prospects to BOMs, but never do it themselves. He/she says things like "Hey, how many people are you bringing Tuesday night to the BOM?" Then when they don't bring anyone, they get frustrated and say to themselves or sideline, upline, "this guy is an idiot, he is not coachable, doesn't want it bad enough!!!"

- A leader is always setting the pace for his team by having new personal prospects at the BOMs and Saturday trainings. They only expect from their team what they are doing themselves. They call their team and say... "Hey I have a new guest coming Tuesday night, what can I do to help you get someone there as well? We are going to do this together! "

- Bosses ask themselves..."Why is my team not getting more people in front of this business?"
- Leaders ask themselves..."How many personal contacts am I going to make this week?"

- Bosses stand in the back of the room or outside of the weekly meeting.
- Leaders sit with their team at the weekly meeting and bring a new prospect.

**In regards to Events...**

- A boss has excuses of why they are not at every event or on every conference call.
- A leader is at every event and on every conference call.

- A boss shows up to the event.
- A leader shows up early and helps put on the event.

- Bosses tell their leaders to get their team to the event. They even send them an email and text.
- Leaders call and promote every event like their lives depend on it. They do 3way calls daily with leaders to new members promoting International, Saturday training, BOM, Leadership trainings, etc. Leaders know that their production completely depends on the amount of people they have at each event. This is what keeps vision, belief, support, training, and unity in their team. This creates success for their reps.

- Bosses send a text out to their team to let them know about the conference call.
- Leaders call everyone on their team and promote the conference call personally.

**In regards to Personal Growth...**

- A manager is always trying to improve and change everyone else around them.
- A leader knows that the only person that they can change and improve is themselves

- A manager says "You" or "I"
- A leader says "We" or "Us"

- A manager cares only about him or herself and his paycheck, not about a relationship.
- A leader truly cares about their team and builds relationships.

- A manager shares negative emotions with his/her team, regardless of the consequences.
- Even when justified, a leader never shows fear, hurt, anger, doubt, frustration to their team. They know it will kill their business. A leader has a positive attitude always. They are uplifting to everyone including sideline and downline. If they have negative feelings or problems this never goes sideline, or downline, it only goes up.

- A boss only sees last month's reports.
- A leader creates belief and vision for their team. They have long-term vision.

- A boss focuses on problems that arise. Problems can easily knock him/her out of the game for a while. Instead of coming up with solutions, they dwell on the problem.
- A leader is solution oriented. They understand that every day they will be faced with problems and without problems there is no business. When problems arise, they call their mentor with a solution already in mind.

- A boss says they are coachable but really just wants validation. When it comes to training or advice, they say "Yep, I knew that, that is what I am doing already!" They get the advice because they asked for it and it was what they needed to hear, but they take any constructive criticism personally and say things like, "He/she doesn't know what they are talking about!"
- A leader is completely coachable. They seek out coaching, not for validation, but only to improve themselves and their business. They are hungry for coaching and ask for constructive criticism. When they get constructive criticism, they don't take it personally, but realize that it was only said out of "love" and so that they can improve their business and themselves. If they don't agree

with the constructive criticism, they still take a good hard look at themselves from a different angle to see what or how they can improve, as it must have been said for a reason...They do everything they can to improve themselves because they know that this is truly the only way they can move forward.

# Chapter Summary

- The cycle of prospecting, presenting the plan, following up, getting customers, and training your team never stops!
- Lead your team by example.
- You aren't the CEO of the company.

*Management activities are ANY activities that aren't producing money.*

Remember that!

# Chapter 15

# SOCIAL MEDIA

There are over 2 billion people with active social media accounts right now in the world. In America alone, over 56% of the population have a profile on a social networking site. Let's just say, there's a lot of people using social media. But there is a wrong way and a right way to use social media for marketing and prospecting your Network Marketing business to your friends and family. The main idea of social media is not to post about your opportunity all the time and firehose your warm market, it's to share key aspects at key times to maximize your piquing and to get someone's contact information. Now, there's sharing key information and then there's sharing any information on social media. Most people will share ANY information, and that will annoy your friends rather than pique their interest about your business. Your business presence in person is also extended to your business presence online and most people aren't using it correctly.

Since there are so many social media platforms out there, I am going to focus on the two biggest ones: Facebook and LinkedIn. When someone on my team tells me that they've run out of names, I say "That's impossible. Get on Facebook." Just to explain very simply, when you create a profile on Facebook and fill out your hometown, your current job, your elementary school, and whatnot, Facebook takes a look through the billions of people using their platform and creates connections between you and others to try and find people you may know. The more information you give to Facebook about you, the more connections it will create with everyone. This works the same way on LinkedIn, except that on there, you're gonna find more business-oriented people. It will sort through resumes and job postings aside from the regular criteria and match people up.

When you post something on Facebook, most people in your friends list will see it (unless they have strict privacy settings, although most people don't.) But friends of your friends will see it too. For example, let's say you and I are friends on Facebook and you post something about your business. I like what I see so I hit the "Like" button. Because I liked your post, someone on MY friends list will see YOUR post. That is called exposure. If you are posting good content in relation to your business and your friends like those things, your exposure could be huge. Something that I strongly recommend is separating your Facebook account into a personal account and a business account. This way, you can use your personal Facebook to talk about how great the new Housewives of whatever show was, and use your business Facebook to promote your business. You will not see Bill Gates post about a drama series on his business page but he may do it to his friends on his personal page. You don't want to confuse people. Now, from time to time, I'll post pictures of myself and my daughter at an amusement park on a Monday morning or photos of me enjoying the lake with my family on a Wednesday afternoon. Those pictures are meant to show the lifestyle that can be made from Network Marketing. It personalizes your business while still promoting your business, and that's fine.

There are three main topics that I recommend staying away from posting onto your business social media: politics, religion, and social matters. If you post onto your business Facebook that you don't like the current President, you have just offended somebody. This is terrible for growing your Network Marketing business. By doing that, you just shut out someone from ever wanting to associate with you, let alone be a part of your business. If you go to a sandwich shop for lunch, they don't care about you being a Democrat or Republican, they just want to sell you a sandwich. Stay away from those touchy subjects because the goal of your Network Marketing business is to recruit the whole world. Don't alienate people before they've had the chance to see your opportunity.

When you create your business Facebook page, make sure to put valuable information in the "About You" or "Bio" section. If somebody invites their friend to check your page out, the first thing they will see is your profile picture. Make sure that it isn't a picture of your dog - your dog isn't gonna make you a millionaire in your Network Marketing business. Make sure to put in some sort of contact information for people to reach out to you. If you post stuff about living the lifestyle, you want interested people to come to you about joining your business. If they can't contact you, how are they gonna get on your team? If your company provides one, put your website relating to your business into your Facebook profile. All this information is a self-edification tool for people that find you online. For example, on my Facebook, I put "Top Money Earner and MLM Guru," and my website, www.angelolvera.com.

Don't become a commercial for your Network Marketing company. If are watching your favorite show, and a commercial comes on at an important point, how annoyed do you get? It's the same thing on social media. If you post every two hours about your service or product, you have become a commercial for your company. Your friends will begin to think, "How many times is this person going to post about their business? I'm gonna have to unfriend them." One business post every week or so is what I do. If something is going on or a new promotion, new millionaire on my team, or someone just got another dream car through my company, maybe I'll post two times a week. But that's it.

What I always try to do is post about something other than myself. I've learned that as you become more and more wealthy, you have to become more and more humble. If someone online sees that you are saying "Thanks to my company and our team, we have another million dollar earner in my group," they'll want to be on your team because you and your team are helping others achieve success. On the contrary, if they see "This is how much money I just withdrew from my account," that makes you look arrogant and like you are just profiting from your team and not helping them.

If you truly feel like you've exhausted most of your warm and lukewarm markets, try cold market recruiting on social media. This has to be done in an effective way or you'll just annoy people. The beauty of social media is that you have access to an incredible number of people whenever you take the time.

If you go on Facebook and start typing 'Car,' you'll get Carol and Carmen. You may know these people or may not know them and that's okay; you're trying to get the whole world on your team. So let's say you click on Carmen Shoemaker and look at her profile. You notice she has a professional picture and then you look through her posts, they lean towards being business oriented. Carmen Shoemaker is a perfect cold market prospect you can send a private message to.

Another way of sending messages to people not on your list is by watching the interactions on your business page. Go ahead and post a congratulations to your kid for making the honor roll at their college on your business page. Let it go as viral as it can and then check through the 'comments' and 'likes' people leave on it. Those 25 - 50 people that interacted with your post are perfect contacts for piquing. Send them a message like:

*"Hey Johnny, thanks for liking my post. Hey listen, if you have kids and are looking for a way to pay for their college, I may have a way to help you do that. Send me your number and I'll get you some information."*

Or, say you post congratulating your sister on her 20th wedding anniversary. You find someone who liked it and send them:

*"Hey Mary, thanks for liking my post. I don't know if you and your spouse would be interested but I have a business where we are showing a lot of couples how to spend more time together and have a better lifestyle. If you're open to a conversation, send me your information."*

Every time someone likes or comments on your posts, that means somebody is watching you on social media. They are taking the time to see what you're doing. That's no different than you walking down the street and someone paying you a nice compliment.

Another way to get prospects is to go through your friends' friends. Here is an example of prospect info I got by messaging a friend's friend:

*Me: Hey Jeffrey, I'm a friend of Elaine's and I saw a comment about you doing what you're passionate about and I thought it was really insightful. I'm developing a company that has great possibilities and a great cash flow, I was wondering if you'd be open to a conversation. If so, send me a number to reach you at.*

*Jeffrey: Hey Angel, would be happy to discuss. I can be reached at xxx-xxx-xxxx.*

Now make sure that you don't go onto social media with the intention of having a conversation online. Don't start talking about your product/service or how great your compensation plan is using your keyboard. Your objective is only to get contact information and add it to your Prospect List. Once you have the name and number, it's business as usual. This method of finding contacts is for when you feel you've exhausted everyone in your network - but really, you haven't. At the end of the day after you've talked to people at the coffee shop or the people in the waiting room while you get your oil in your car changed, you can use social media to prospect when you aren't face to face with people.

And remember, when you contact someone on social media, what do you think is the first thing they're gonna do? Check YOUR profile. This is why you need a professional business profile that lets people know that you are a serious entrepreneur. They see your team earning residual income, your team earning company cars, you at the lake in your houseboat on a Wednesday and they feel like they would be stupid not to talk to you.

# DIGITAL BILLBOARDS

#Hashtags.

## WHAT IS A HASHTAG?

A hashtag is a keyword or phrase with the pound symbol (#) in front that people include in their social media posts. Essentially, it makes the content of your post accessible to all people with similar interests, even if they're not your followers or fans. For example, let's say you're an Apple fan and that you're trying to decide on buying an iPhone 6s. A simple "#iPhone6s" search on any social network will open a dedicated news feed with all iPhone 6s latest updates, deals, rumors and hacks. The results you see on this feed are the most recent and most popular posts of any users who used "# iPhone6s" in their posts. But usually, users don't actively search for hashtags, they simply spot them. Hashtags appear as clickable links on posts, and clicking on it will display a real-time live feed of every other post tagged with the same hashtag.

## WHY ARE THEY USEFUL?

Assuming your social media profile is public, using hashtags makes your posts visible to basically anyone who shares your interest. Think of it as a Digital Billboard. No longer are your posts limited to just your followers; your content is now accessible to all other users interested in similar topics. Choosing the right hashtag can greatly broaden the reach of your social media posts to thousands of potential followers, fans or customers.

## WHAT DO I DO?

I have provided a list here of a mix of Network Marketing-related and popular hashtags. You can use these on your social media posts and they will make your SUCCESS posts more visible to the public and pique interest of anyone just skimming through stuff online. You can just copy and paste these into your posts BUT remember this important fact about HASHTAG LIMITS:

INSTAGRAM and FACEBOOK ALLOW A MAX OF 30 HASHTAGS (at the time of this writing).

If you add more than 30, your ENTIRE text will NOT show up and you have to type EVERYTHING again (it's happened to me too many times, #frustrating)

You can use up to 30 hashtags but you'll get the best results if you stick to anywhere between 5-10. A billboard is good for advertising but how many would you have to see from the same company to annoy you?

## GOOD HASHTAGS FOR NETWORKERS

#business #ihatemondays #ihatemyjob #planb #entrepreneur #stayathomemom #jobssuck #financialfreedom #travel #payoffdebt #payoffbills #payoffloans #millionairemindset #lifestyle #lifeisgood #lifestylechange #change #happy #SmallBusiness #healthyliving #myjobsucks #smile #amazing

A good resource I have found for checking out the popularity of hashtags is ritetag.com/hashtag-search Using that site, you can search millions of hashtags and figure out how popular they are and who is using them in what social media platform.

Happy hashtagging!

# Chapter Summary

- The main idea of social media is to share key aspects at key times to maximize your piquing.
- Your business presence in person is extended to your business presence online.
- Separate your Facebook account into a personal account and a business account.
- It's ok to post pictures of you at the lake on a weekday, it makes you look down to earth and promotes your business results at the same time.
- Every time someone likes or comments on your posts, that means somebody is watching you on social media.
- When you contact someone on social media, they are going to check your profile, so make sure that has relevant info.
- Use #hashtags to reach a broader audience.
- DON'T FIREHOSE PEOPLE!

## Chapter 16

# NEXT STEPS

Do another 90 days! In this business, your first 90 days don't necessarily start when you first sign up. They start when you decide that what you have been doing isn't working and you need to learn to do it the right way. Sometimes, our egos get in the way of being coachable, and when our uplines see that, they give up on us. Well, your downline will give up on you too! Hopefully you can use the skills in this book to change the way you manage your business and make it profitable as soon as possible. Take all the tips in this book, along with the system your uplines have spent years creating, and duplicate it out to your team to make sure you're on the path to success.

# CREDITS AND ATTRIBUTION

Apple® and iPhone6s® are registered trademarks of Apple Inc.

www.ritetag.com is the exclusive property of RiteTag and its licensors.

"Facebook" is a registered trademark of Facebook, Inc.

The Instagram name and logo are trademarks of Instagram.

For all credits and attributions,
All Rights are Reserved.

# NOTES

# NOTES

# Angel Olvera

Visit my website at www.angelolvera.com and put in your info to stay informed about any future books and trainings.

You can also reach me by email at business@angelolvera.com

If this book was of benefit to you, please email me a review and I promise to post the FULL review you give me, unedited and unaltered in any way, on areas of the internet and in print where reviews are relevant.

Thank you for reading and I'll see you at the top!

CPSIA information can be obtained
at www.ICGtesting.com
Printed in the USA
LVHW082349190919
631611LV00021B/1216/P